AF587966

PEGASUS ENCYCLOPEDIA LIBRARY

DISCOVERIES AND INVENTIONS

COMPUTERS

Edited by: Anil Kumar Tomar, Pallabi B. Tomar
Managing editor: Tapasi De
Designed by: Vijesh Chahal, Anil Kumar, Rohit Kumar
Illustrated by: Suman S. Roy, Tanoy Choudhury
Colouring done by: Vinay Kumar, Sonu, Kiran Kumari & Pradeep Kumar

CONTENTS

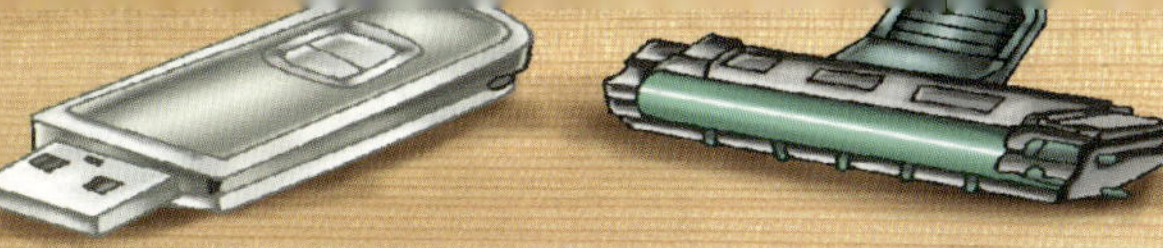

What is a computer?

The word computer was devised for a computing machine which can perform calculations on large numerical data. It is an electronic device that receives data and a set of instructions, processes the data as per provided instructions and provides output in the form of information. In today's world, computers are an essential part of everyday life and perform a wide range of tasks. They are used everywhere throughout society in the storage and handling of data, from homes to offices, schools and colleges to research centres, secret governmental files to banking transactions.

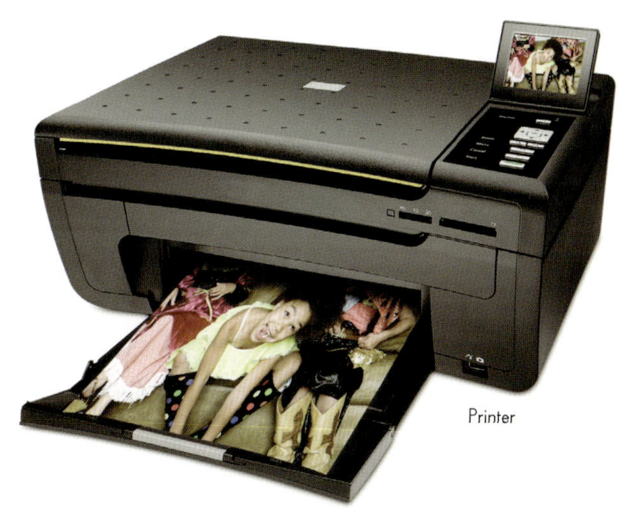

Printer

Monitor

Processor (computer)

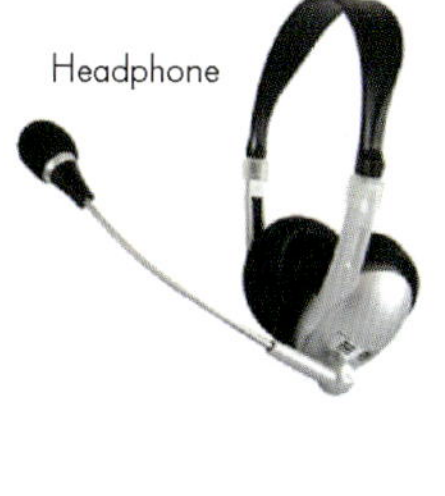

Headphone

PC Camera

Speaker

Keyboard

Mouse

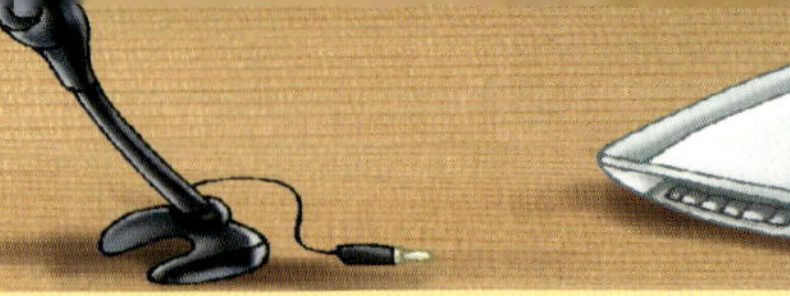

Characteristics of a computer

Diligence

A computer is free from monotony, tiredness, lack of concentration etc. It can continuously repeat the same work for number of times without getting bored and can work for long hours without getting tired.

Versatility

A computer is a versatile machine and can perform various tasks of different fields at the same time. The same system can be used for calculations, entertainment, education and many other works.

Accuracy

A computer always provides an accurate result. Errors can occur, but these are mainly human created due to wrong input of data and instructions. Computers do not have their own brain thus generally regarded as 'GIGO' that means garbage in garbage out.

Astonishing fact

Sweden is the country with the highest percentage of Internet users (75 per cent).

Brief history of computers

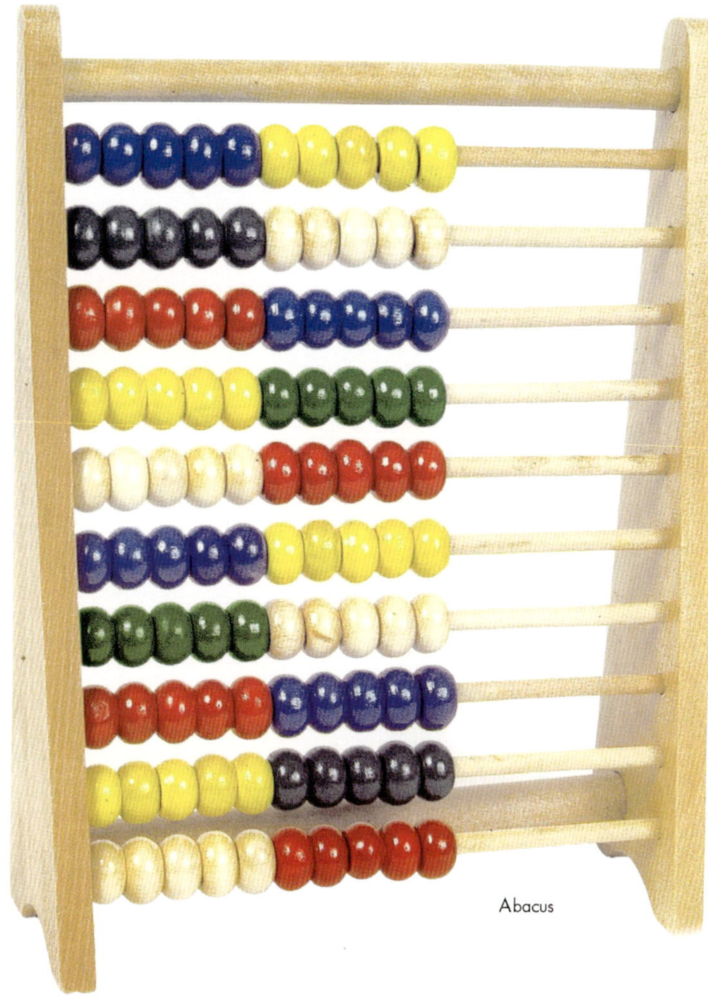
Abacus

Ancient Times: Abacus is the earliest known device used for computations. It dates back to ancient times and was invented by the Chinese. Ten beads strung onto wires attached to a frame were devised for addition and subtraction of small numbers. This device is still used in play schools to teach kids.

17th Century: John Napier devised a system, known as Napier's bones where he put the logarithms on a set of ivory rods. By sliding the numbers up and down, he invented a very primitive slide rule and this marks the beginning of logarithms.

1642: Blaise Pascal developed the first real calculator. This calculator was devised to carry out additions and subtractions by using a series of very light rotating wheels.

Astonishing fact

The command 'Ctrl+Alt+Delete' was written by David Bradley.

Pascal's calculator

Jacquard loom

Difference engine

1690: Gottfried van Leibnitz developed a calculating machine that could add, subtract, multiply and divide.

1834: Joseph Jacquard developed punched cards to control the loom patterns. These cards were programmed with instructions and are considered as the ancestor of the IBM punched cards for information storage.

1812: Charles Babbage designed and built the **difference engine**. In 1833, he also designed a machine capable of any type of calculation and called it the **analytic engine**. Babbage is known as the father of the modern day computers.

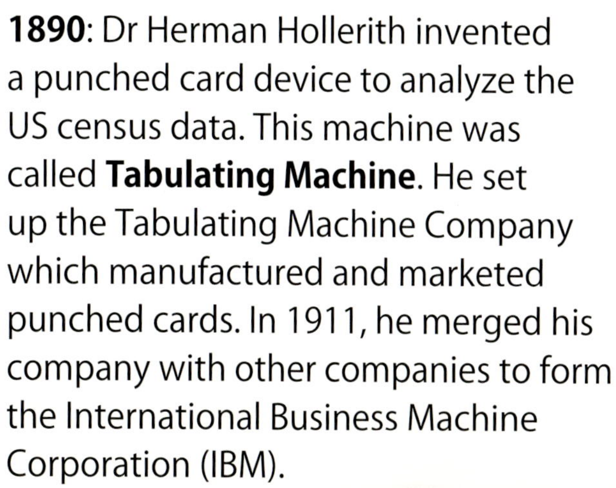

1890: Dr Herman Hollerith invented a punched card device to analyze the US census data. This machine was called **Tabulating Machine**. He set up the Tabulating Machine Company which manufactured and marketed punched cards. In 1911, he merged his company with other companies to form the International Business Machine Corporation (IBM).

1944: Howard Aiken devised the first automatic calculator, Mark I, through collaboration with Harvard University, IBM, and the U.S. War Department.

1945: Jon Von Neumann developed the first stored-program computer, the EDVAC (Electronic Discrete Variable Automatic Computer). This machine marked the beginning of the computer age.

Tabulating Machine

The EDVAC was built for the U.S. Army's Ballistics Research Laboratory by the University of Pennsylvania. The computer that was built was to be binary with automatic addition, subtraction, multiplication, programmed division and automatic checking with a memory capacity of 1,000 words. Physically EDVAC had almost 6,000 vacuum tubes and 12,000 diodes. It consumed 56 kw of power. It covered 490 ft^2 of floor and weighed almost 7,850 kg! The typical operating personnel were thirty people for each eight-hour shift.

1946: J. Presper Eckert and John W. Mauchly invented the first electronic computer 'ENIAC' (Electronic Numerical Integrator and Calculator).

Types of computers

Computers are broadly divided into two groups depending on the type of data they process— analog computers and digital computers.

Astonishing fact

One of the world's leading computer and computer peripheral manufacturer Hewlett Packard was first started in a garage at Palo Alto in the year 1939.

Analog computers

Analog computers do arithmetic and logical operations by processing continuous physical data such as temperature, pressure, weight, power density or voltage. These computers use analog signals as input and output source. They utilize mechanical, hydraulic or electrical energy for operation. They are only special purpose computers.

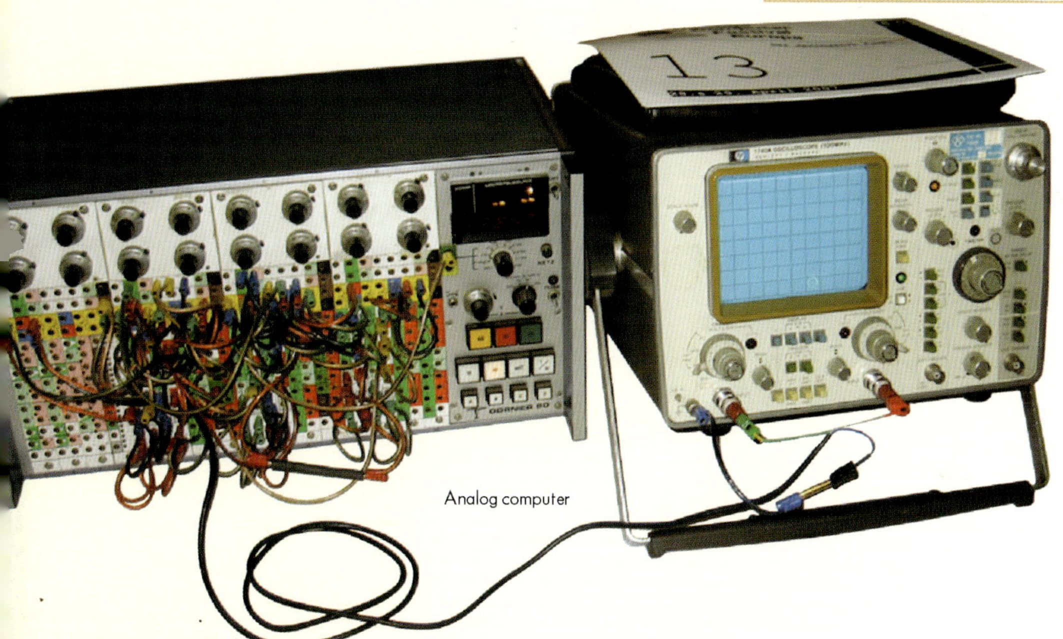

Analog computer

Digital computers

Digital computers use digital signals to process the data. They work on the principles of binary mathematics where everything is represented by binary numbers (0 and 1). Most of the modern day computers are digital computers.

Digital computer

Based on capacity, speed and reliability, computers can be classified into four categories.

Micro computers

These are the most common and abundant computers which are also known as Personal Computers. These are single user machines which have less memory and slow processing speed. These are most popular computers due to their small size and low cost. Personal computers are of many types and some of them are desktops, work stations, notebooks, tablet computers, and handheld computers etc.

Mini computers

Mini computers are small in size and have low processing speed with capabilities between the range of a personal desktop computer and a mainframe. These computers are used in small offices, government departments and educational institutes where small networking is required to connect several terminals. These computers are commonly used as network servers. Single user mini computers are also used for some specific tasks by researchers, designers, engineers etc.

Super computers

A super computer is the most powerful, fastest and most expensive type of computer systems which can perform trillions of calculations per second! It consists of large number of processors connected together for parallel processing. It is used to process large amount of data and to solve the complicated scientific problems. Super computers are mainly used in large organizations, research laboratories, aerospace centres, large industrial units etc. Some of the important purposes are weather forecasting, analysis of nuclear reactions, predicting the interactions of millions of atoms, aircraft designing, automotive design, and online banking etc. Some of the super computers are CRAY series, PARAM and ETA A-10 etc.

Mainframe computers

Mainframes are large and high-performance powerful computer systems to handle the processing of thousands of users at same the time. These computers are large in size, highly expensive and have high processing speed.

How does a computer work?

A computer should always consist of input device, central processing unit (CPU), storage device and output device. The data and instructions are given by user through input devices like keyboard. CPU is the brain of computers where all the processing tasks are performed. CPU processes the data step by step according to provided user instructions. The processed data is called information which is visualized by output unit such as Visualizing Display Unit (VDU) which is commonly known as Monitor.

Astonishing fact

The first Apple computer was built by Steve Jobs and Steve Wozniak. It was made by using parts they got for free from their employers!

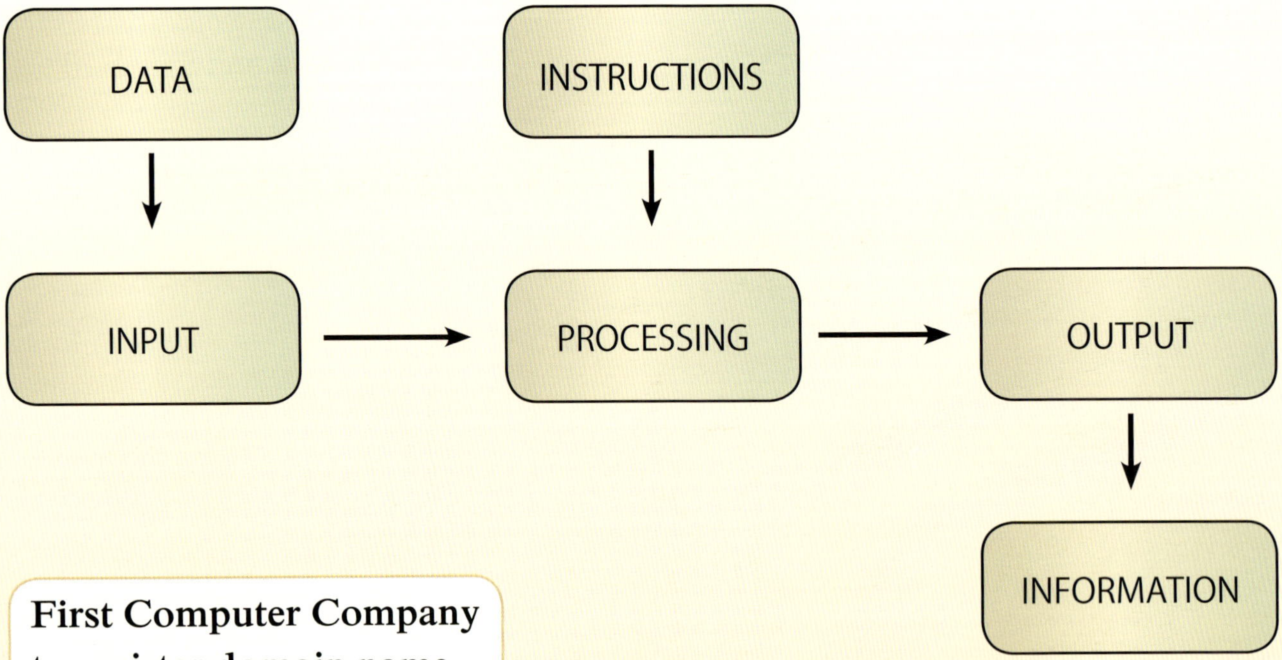

DATA → INPUT

INSTRUCTIONS → PROCESSING

INPUT → PROCESSING → OUTPUT

OUTPUT → INFORMATION

First Computer Company to register domain name was 'Digital Equipment Corporation'.

Input devices

A computer user enters data, commands and programs into the CPU using input devices. The main function of input devices is to convert human understandable signals into the machine language. Each entry from keyboard is converted into binary codes (a string of 0 and 1). The most common input device is the keyboard. Other important input devices are mouse, light pen, joysticks, scanners, digital camera, optical character recognition (OCR) devices, Magnetic ink character recognition (MICR) devices, touch screens, microphones and many more. The storage devices (CD, DVD, pen drive, hard disk etc.) can also be used to input data.

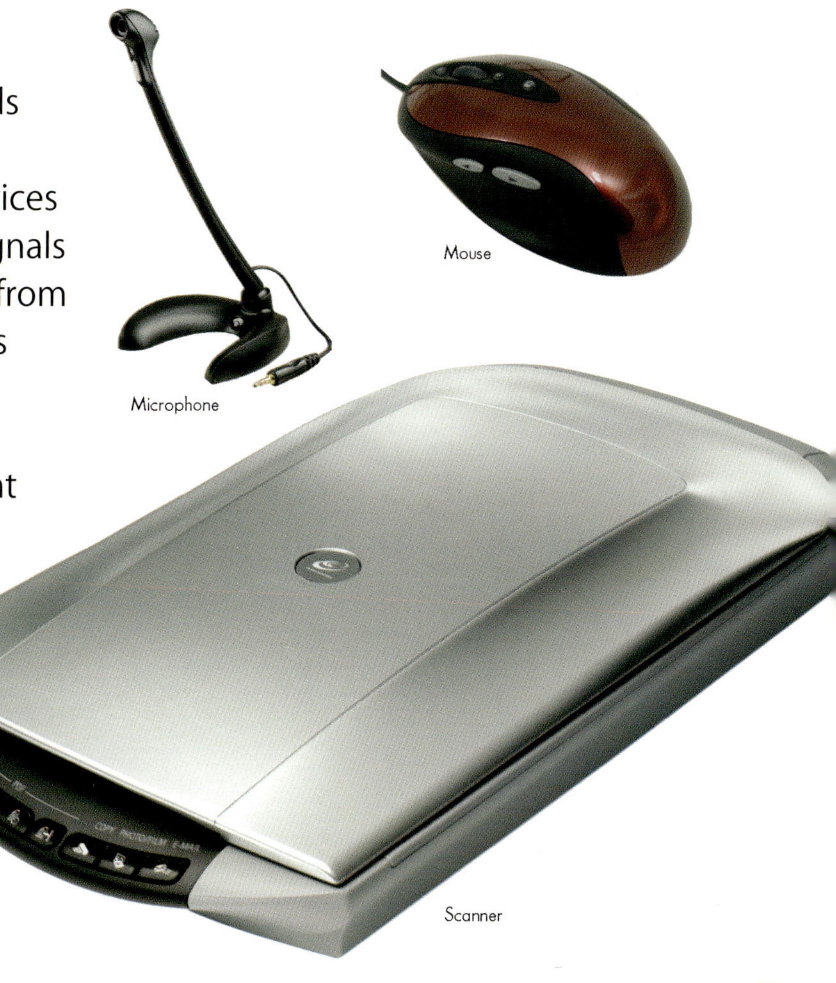

Mouse

Microphone

Scanner

Keyboard

First hard disk drive was introduced by Seagate in 1979, which could hold 5 M.B. of data.

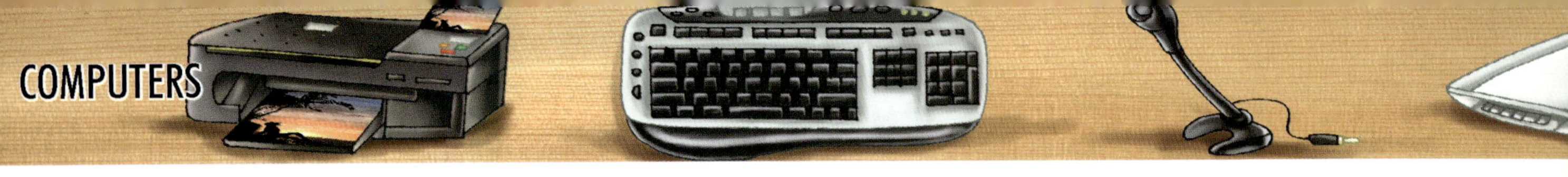

Central Processing Unit

The CPU is the main functional unit of a computer system. It performs arithmetic and logical calculations and also controls the operations of other system elements. All operations are performed by specific integrated circuits (ICs). These circuits are integrated on a chip which is known as a **Microprocessor**. Microprocessors are used in most of today's personal computers.

The CPU consists of three major functional units which are connected through internal buses.

- Memory unit or registers
- Control unit
- Arithmetic/Logic unit

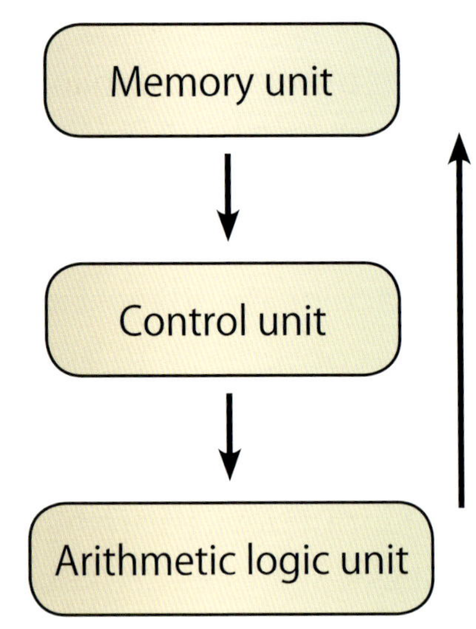

Memory unit/Registers

All the user instructions and input data are temporarily stored in the registers. Thus, registers are also known as temporary storage areas. The major functions of this unit are:

- Registers hold the input data which will be processed.
- Registers also keep the track of user instructions.
- They store intermediate results which are used in the next step of instructions as input.
- They keep the address of storage locations of results.

Control unit

The control unit is one of the most important units for better functioning of a computer system. This unit controls all the operations of a system. The main functions of this unit include:

- This unit distributes CPU time for different operations.
- It regulates execution of all the operations.
- It also reads the patterns of data in a designated register and translates the pattern into an activity.
- This unit decides the order in which all the operations will be performed.

Arithmetic/Logic Unit

The arithmetic/logic unit gives the chip its calculating ability and permits arithmetical and logical operations.

Internal bus

Internal bus is a network of communication wires that connects all the internal units of the CPU with each other and also with the external components of a computer system. These buses are classified as the following:

- Control Bus is used by a CPU for communicating with other devices within the computer.
- Address Bus is a one way connection that handles the location of data in memory addresses.
- Data Bus reads data from memory and writes new data into memory. This is a two way communication line.

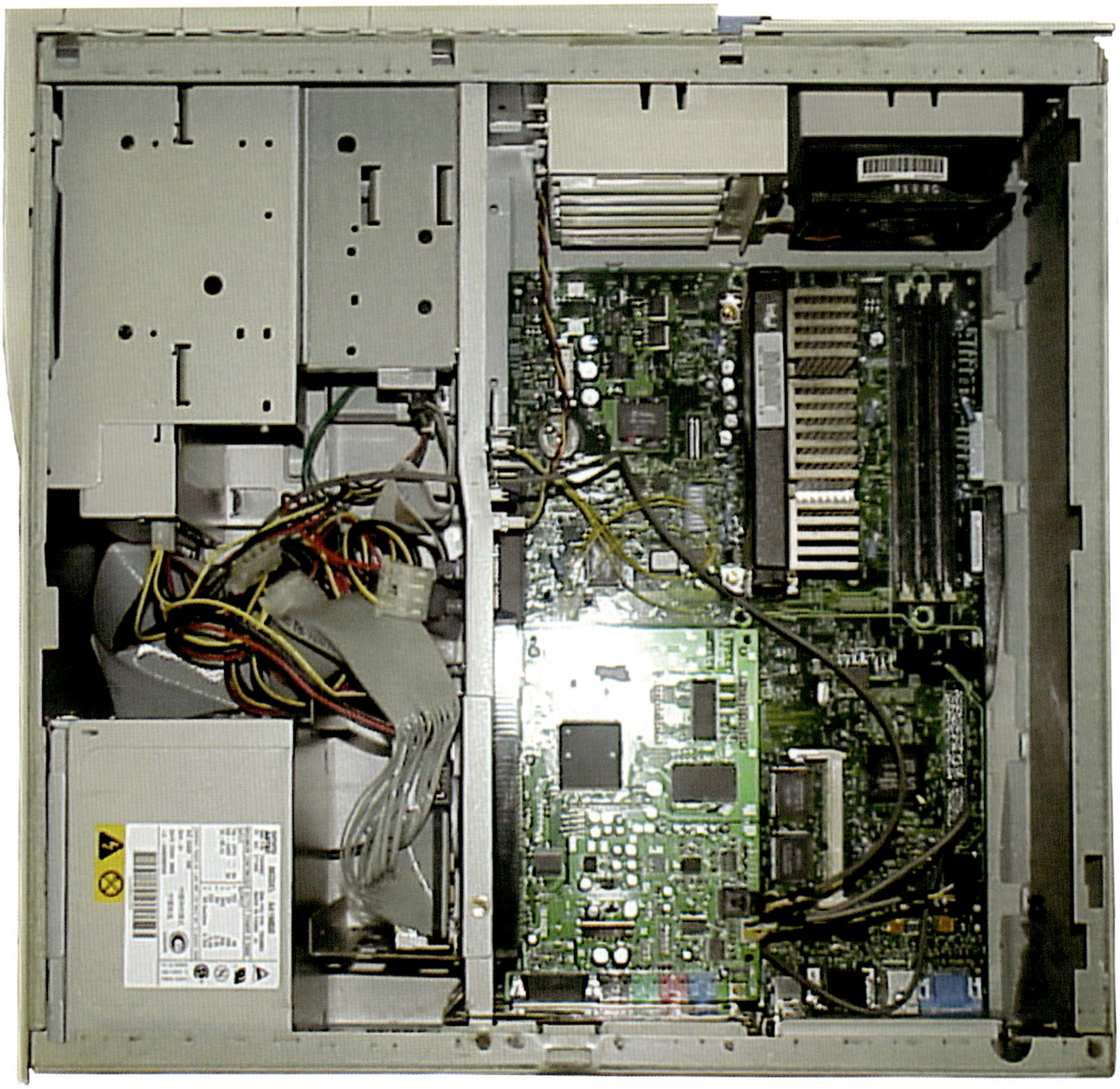

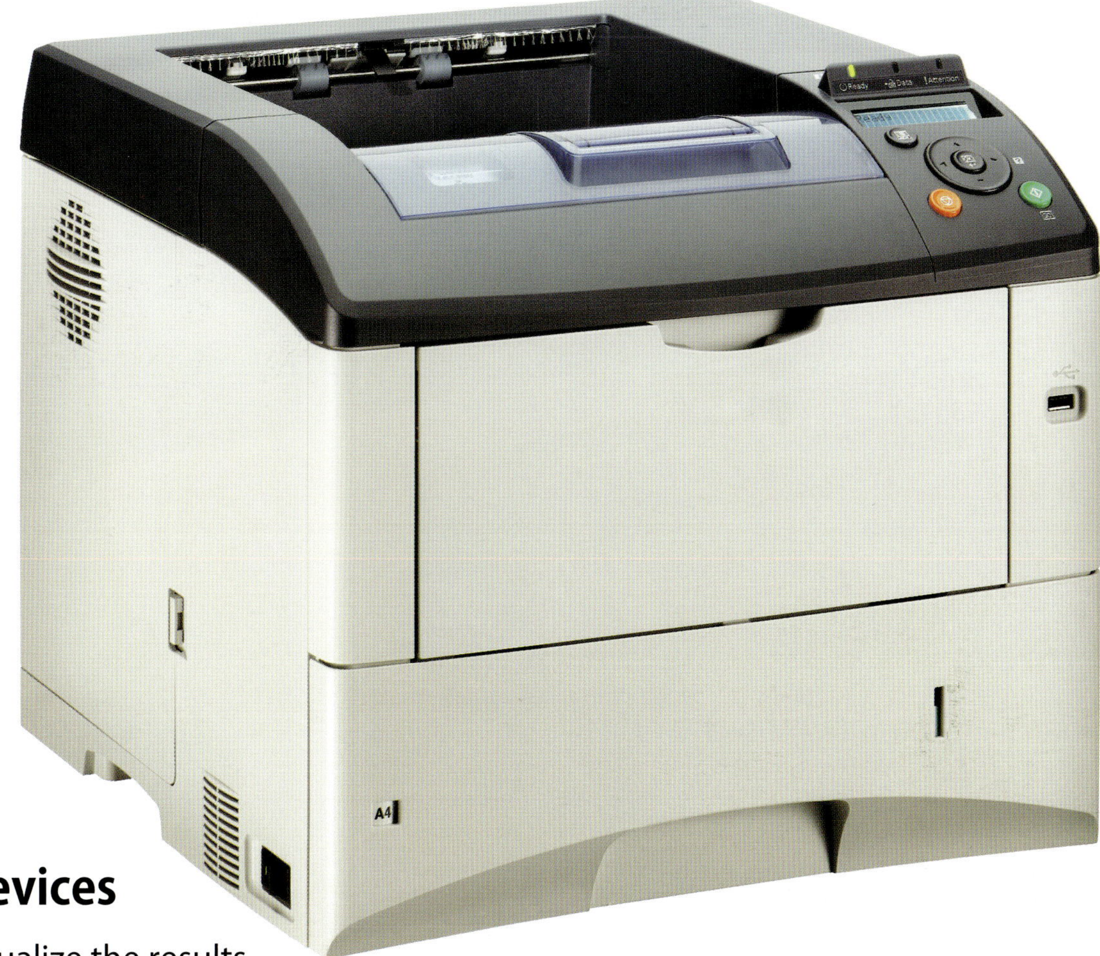

Output devices

A user can visualize the results of data processed by CPU by output devices. The main function of output devices is to convert the results into human understandable form from machine language. The most common output device is Video Display unit (VDU) which is also known as monitor. A monitor displays characters and graphics on a television-like screen. Other output devices are printers, plotters, speakers and secondary storage devices etc.

Printers

Printers are commonly used output devices connected to computer system to print text and graphics on the plain papers. There are many types of printers to fulfill the requirements of the specific user. The most commonly used printers are:

- Dot-matrix Printer
- Inkjet Pinter
- Laser Printer

Dot-matrix printers create characters by striking pins against an ink ribbon. Each pin makes a dot and combinations of dots form characters and illustrations. They are noisy and very slow in comparison to inkjet and laser printers.

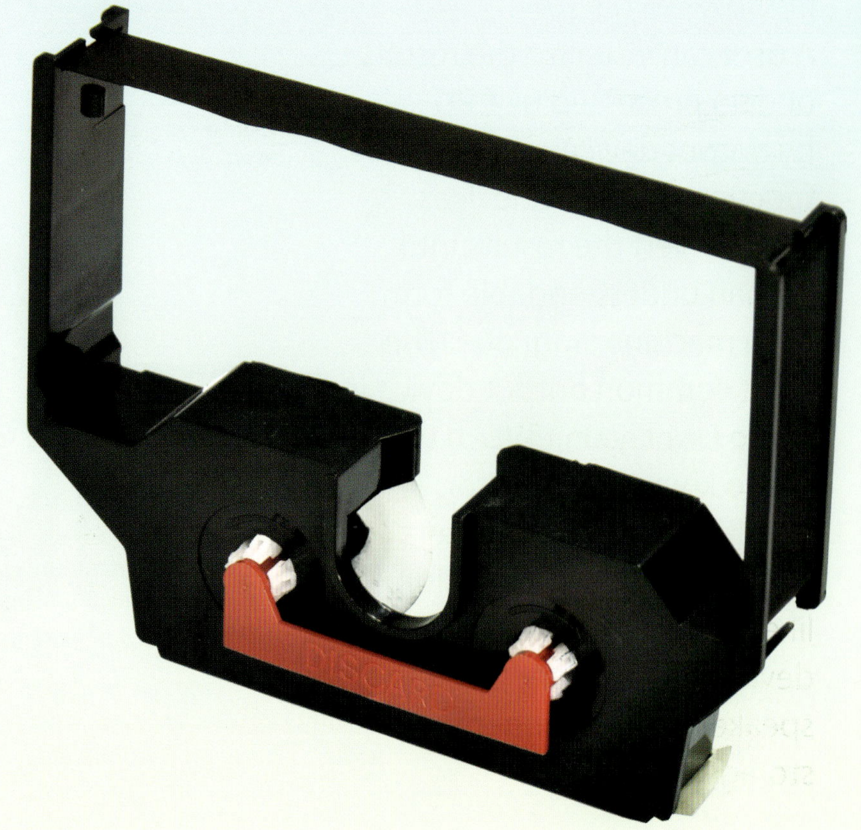

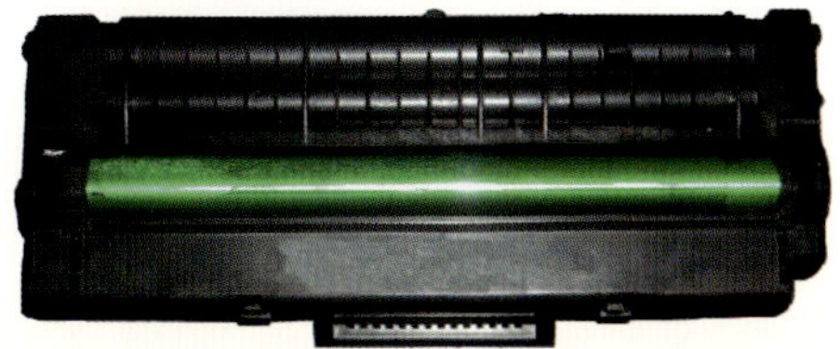

Inkjet printers work by propelling variably-sized droplets of liquid or molten material (ink) onto almost any medium. They are the most common type of printers for domestic purposes due to their low cost and high quality of output. These printers are very easy to use and handle. The main disadvantage is that the printing is slow, little noisy and non-economical.

Laser printers use LED-technology to obtain small particles of toner from a cartridge onto paper. They produce high quality text and graphics on plain paper. The printing is fast and more economical than of inkjet printers.

Computer memory

Computer memory is basically a place where data and instructions are stored in any form electronic, magnetic or optical. It is generally categorized into volatile memory and non-volatile memory according to the storage type. The volatile memory needs to be supplied with external power in order to hold and refresh data while a non-volatile memory can maintain data for extended periods of time without any power being supplied to the device. Thus, volatile memory is preferred for high-speed processing and short-term access while for long term storage and future access non-volatile memory is preferred. Random Access Memory (RAM) and Read Only Memory (ROM) constitute computers' internal memory as they are integrated part of processor circuit. The secondary storage devices like hard disk, magnetic tapes, zip drives, floppy disk drives and optical storage media are known as computer's external memory. They may or may not physically reside within processing unit but are not mounted on the main circuit.

Random access memory

Random access memory or RAM is the main memory of a computer system used for storing user instructions and data. It is volatile and provides temporary read/write storage. As soon as the power is turned off, all the data is lost. It is expensive and fast with access times generally less than nanoseconds. Every data and program is first stored in RAM for execution by CPU. RAM may be further divided into two categories:

Static random access memory (SRAM)

This type of RAM retains the data as long as power is available. It is fast and expensive and is used to create speed sensitive cache.

Dynamic random access memory (DRAM)

Dynamic RAM has to be dynamically refreshed all of the time. It is less expensive and slower and is used for larger RAM space requirements.

Read only memory

All computers contain a non-volatile read-only memory (ROM) that holds instructions for starting up the computer or a specific program. In general, ROM memory is used to hold and make available instructions that cannot be altered by users. Instructions are programmed into ROM memory during fabrication. According to data storage format, ROM can be divided into one-time programmable ROM (OTPROM), erasable programmable ROM (EPROM), electrically erasable programmable ROM (EEPROM) and many others.

Did you know that 'Stewardesses' is the longest word which can be typed with only the left hand?

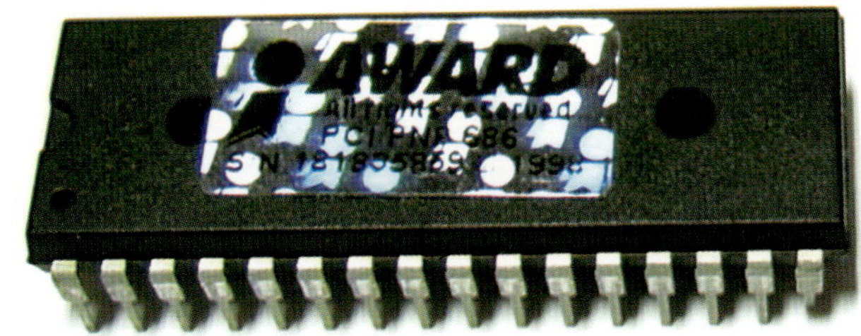

Secondary storage devices

The secondary storage is known as peripheral storage, and is used to store information of the computer that is not in current use. This is typically slower due to serial access and is of higher capacity than primary storage. The secondary storage devices are non-volatile. The common secondary storage devices are hard disks, optical drive such as CDs or DVDs and USB flash drives. The optical drives use lasers to store and read data on CDs and DVDs. USB flash drives are easily portable and have become incredibly popular due to the very small size compared to the amount of data these can store.

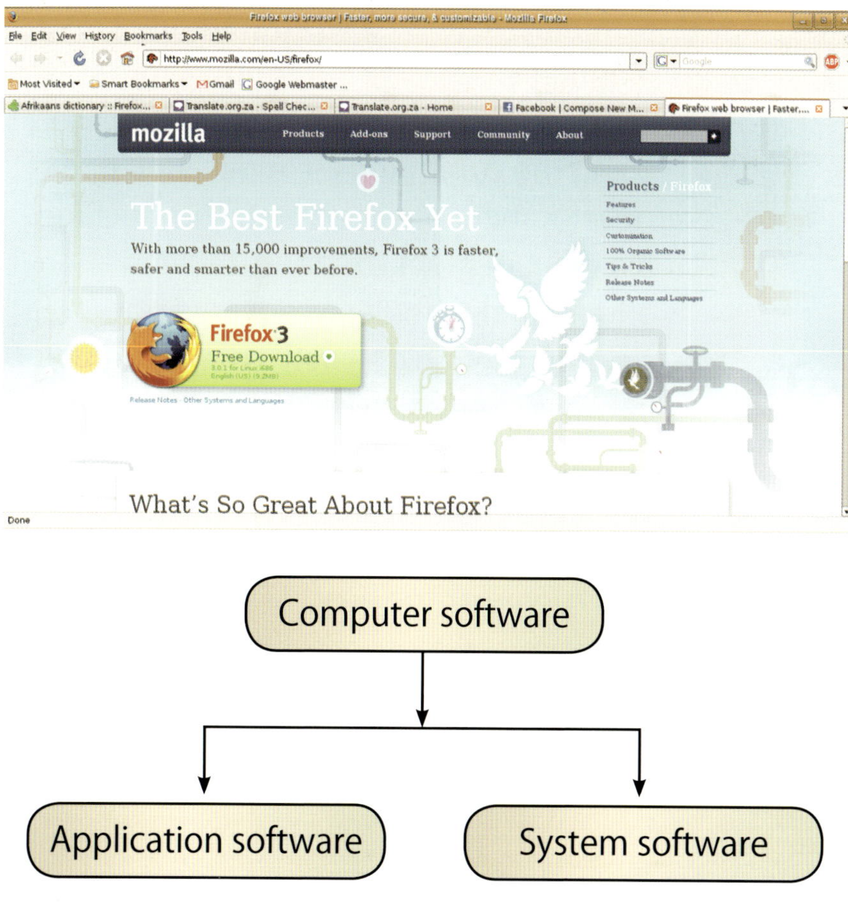

Computer Software are the programs are the intermediate link between computer system and user which aid to the proper functioning of the hardware of the computer system and support end user computing.

Application software

These are the programs developed for general-purpose or specific applications. These programs perform common information processing jobs for end users. Some of the common general-purpose programs are software suits, word processor, spreadsheet, web browsers, database managers, telecommunications, and graphics programs. Specific application programs include engineering and science applications for research and development purpose, educational and learning packages, statistical tools and business applications.

System software

These programs manage and support operations of a computer system for data processing tasks. System management programs manage the hardware, software, networks and other components of a computer system during its execution of information processing jobs. They include operating system, diagnostic tools, compilers, servers, data communication programs, database management systems, system utility programs and performance monitors etc. Development programs include the programming language tools and translators etc. The system utility programs support using the computer, an application or a development environment. They include file management (creating, moving and renaming folders, copying and deleting files), file search, comparing file contents. They also include software for performing diagnostic routines to check the performance and current health of the hardware. The operating system is considered as the head of the system software and most of the other system softwares are installed with it.

Operating systems

An operating system is integration of system programs that supervises and manages all of the CPU operations, controls the input/output storage functions of the computer system and provides various support services. It runs all the time and serves as the head of the computer system. It provides the environment where all the programs and software can only be executed. Thus, the basic function of an operating system is to create an interface between system and user. The popular operating systems are Windows 2000, XP, Windows 7, MS-DOS, Macintosh OS, OS/2, UNIX, Linux, Fedora, Ubuntu and many others.

It is believed that the first computer virus released in the world was a boot sector virus, which was created in the year 1986 by Farooq Alvi brothers. It was designed by them to protect their research work.

Number system

We use decimal number system in our routine calculations. It has base 10 and all the numbers are represented by 10 digits (0, 1, 2, 3, 4, 5, 6, 7, 8 and 9). The commonly used number systems used by computers are binary, octal and hexadecimal. Most of the personal computer systems use binary number systems.

Binary number system has base 2 and the representing digits are 0 and 1. These digits are known as Binary Digits (BITS). **Octal number system** has base 8 and representing digits are 0-7 while **hexadecimal number system** has base 16 and representing symbols are 0-9 and A-F.

Measurement units of computer memory

Computer memory or storage capacity is measured by Binary Digits (0 and 1). This

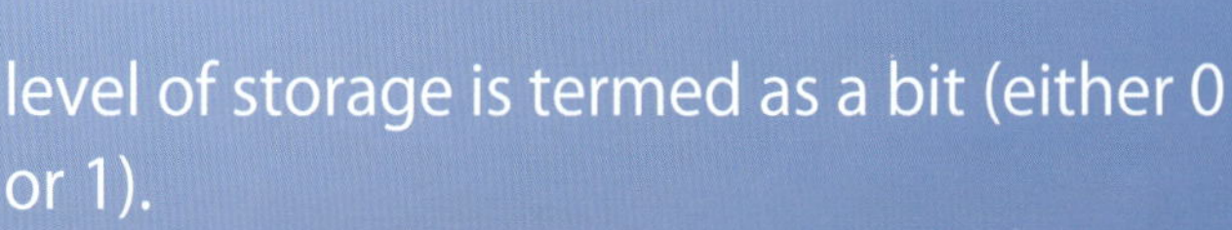

level of storage is termed as a bit (either 0 or 1).

1 byte	=	8 bits
1kilobyte (KB)	=	1024 bytes
1megabyte (MB)	=	1024 kilobytes
1gigabyte (GB)	=	1024 megabyte
1terabyte (TB)	=	1024 gigabyte

Decimal	Binary	Octal	Hexadecimal
0	0	0	0
1	1	1	1
2	10	2	2
3	11	3	3
4	100	4	4
5	101	5	5
6	110	6	6
7	111	7	7
8	1000	10	8
9	1001	11	9
10	1010	12	A
11	1011	13	B
12	1100	14	C
13	1101	15	D
14	1110	16	E
15	1111	17	F

Internet

Internet is the network of networks which connects computer systems worldwide by various means such as telephone wires or satellite. The www (**World Wide Web**) is a network of sites that can be searched and retrieved by a special protocol known as a Hypertext Transfer protocol (HTTP). This protocol searches the address on the web and automatically retrieves for viewing.

Milestones to the discovery of Internet Technology

1973: The Internet technology was developed by Vinton Cerf in 1973 as part of a United States Department of Defense Advanced Research Projects Agency (DARPA) project. The computer network this project produced was called ARPANET that linked U.S. scientific and academic researchers.

1974: ARPA scientists, working closely with experts in Stanford, developed a common language that would allow different networks to communicate with each other. This was known as a transmission control protocol/internet protocol (TCP/IP).

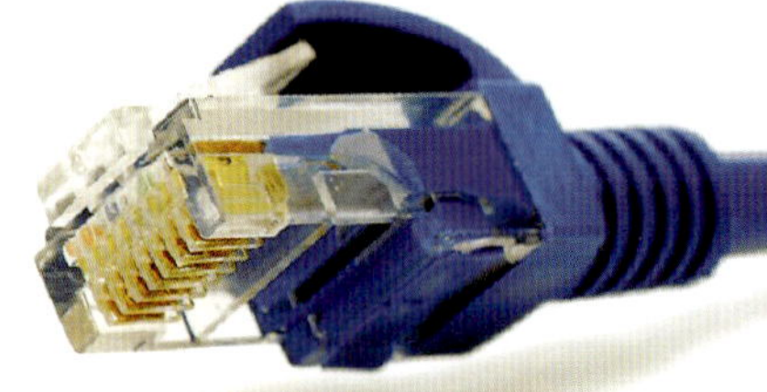

Google Chrome BETA

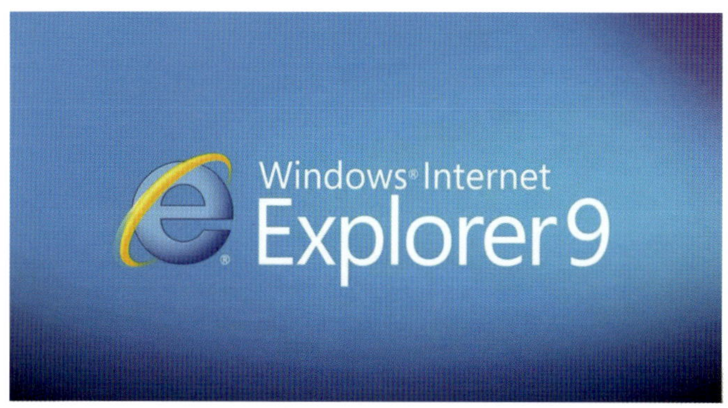

1989: Tim Berners-Lee and scientists at CERN (Geneva) designed **WWW concept** in 1989 for making data retrieval process easier. He also developed a 'browser/ editor' program and called it **World Wide Web**.

1990: Archie, the first Internet search-engine for finding and retrieving computer files was developed at McGill University, Montreal.

1991: World Wide Web (internet) was released to the public.

How does the internet work?

Internet Network can be divided into two groups— servers and browsers. **Servers** store most of the information on the internet. They share this information with other servers and make it available for browsers. **Browsers** are standard computer systems which access the stored information on servers through web browsers. Some of the popular web browsers are Netscape Navigator, Microsoft Internet Explorer, Mozilla Firefox, Google Chrome and Opera etc.

Computer viruses

Computer viruses are the programs which are designed for self replication by infecting the executable files, system areas or storage media without the knowledge of the user. The most common mode of infection these days is internet. The actions and effects are most of the times considered bad ranging from mild disturbance to high damages to the system and its components. The notorious virus irritate users by flashing silly messages or product advertising while harmful virus can delete or corrupt important system files as well as stored data. The common types of virus are trojan horses, worms, parasites, hoaxes, macros, and boot sector viruses etc.

Trojan horses: These are malicious program codes which are not self-replicative. They are always spread in the form of good offers and once clicked; they spread rapidly and infect the complete system. These are one of the most common types of virus.

Hoaxes: These are the email messages carrying wrong information and instruction. Sometimes they are coded for self forwarding. Once these messages are opened, they are forwarded to everyone in the address book.

Boot sector viruses: These viruses install themselves on the beginning tracks of hard drives. They are malicious in nature and corrupt the device.

Test Your MEMORY

1. What are the main characteristics of a computer system?
2. Who is known as the father of computers and why?
3. What are the different types of computers?
4. What are the input and output devices?
5. Write a short note on Central Processing Unit?
6. What is the difference between volatile and non-volatile memories?
7. What are secondary storage devices?
8. Name some of the common operating system?
9. Classify the computer softwares.
10. How does the internet work?
11. What are the different types of printers?
12. What are the common types of computer viruses?

Index